Totally AMAZING FACTS ABOUT CATS

NIKKI POTTS

raintree

a Capstone company — publishers for children

WILD CATS

DATE BACK TO PREHISTORIC TIMES.

 sabre-toothed tiger

DOMESTICATED CATS HAVE BEEN AROUND FOR ABOUT 8,000 YEARS.

One legend says cats were created when a lion on **NOAH'S ARK** sneezed and **TWO KITTENS** came out!

ANCIENT EGYPTIANS THOUGHT CATS WERE MAGICAL CREATURES.

Ancient Egyptians believed **GODDESS BASTET** had the power to **TRANSFORM** herself into a **CAT**.

In **1888**, hundreds of thousands of MUMMIFIED CATS were discovered in an Egyptian burial ground.

ANCIENT EGYPTIANS MOURNED THE DEATH OF A FAMILY CAT BY SHAVING OFF THEIR EYEBROWS.

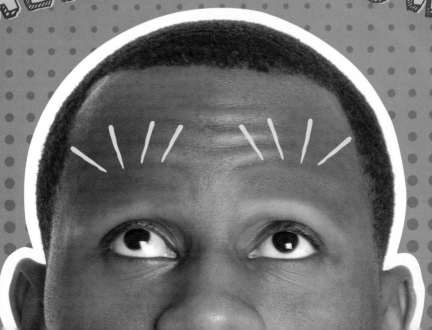

The EGYPTIAN MAU is one of the OLDEST cat breeds.

THERE ARE MORE THAN **35** BREEDS OF WILD CATS.

12

The RUSTY-SPOTTED CAT is the SMALLEST WILD CAT.

It weighs about the same as a **PINEAPPLE**, at just 1–1.6 kilograms (2.2–3.5 pounds).

THE MAINE COON IS THE OFFICIAL CAT OF THE US STATE OF MAINE.

Greetings FROM MAINE USA

14

A MAINE COON CAN WEIGH ALMOST 9 KILOGRAMS (20 POUNDS).

That's as much as a dining room chair!

BENGALS
ARE A MIX OF

ASIAN
LEOPARD
CATS
AND
DOMESTIC
CATS.

16

Most BENGALS love water.

THE WORLD'S LONGEST

DOMESTIC CAT WAS A MAINE COON CALLED

MYMAINS STEWART GILLIGAN.

HE WAS

123 CENTIMETRES
(48.3 INCHES) LONG.

A DOMESTIC CAT set a RECORD SPEED of nearly 50 KILOMETRES (30 MILES) PER HOUR!

The **OLDEST** cat lived to be

38 YEARS

AND 3 DAYS OLD.

That's about **170** in human years!

A millionaire left

7 MILLION POUNDS

to his cat, BLACKIE, when he died.

ACCORDING TO GUINNESS WORLD RECORDS, THE MOST EXPENSIVE CAT WAS PURCHASED FOR

£15,925.

CATS can make more than 100 SOUNDS.

Most ADULT CATS only

MEOW

to communicate with HUMANS.

A CAT CAN RECOGNIZE ITS OWNER'S VOICE.

BUT it often chooses to **IGNORE** it!

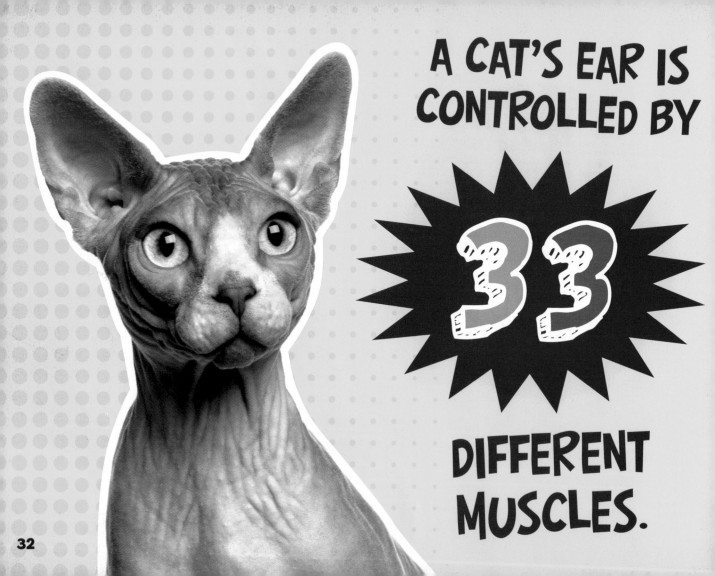

A CAT'S EAR IS CONTROLLED BY **33** DIFFERENT MUSCLES.

Cats can move their ears 180 DEGREES, and separately.

CATS CAN
HEAR SOUNDS
UP TO ABOUT

64 kHz.

HUMANS can only **HEAR** up to about **20 KHz.**

ALL CATS CAN RETRACT THEIR CLAWS

except for the cheetah!

CHEETAHS are the FASTEST mammals.

THEY CAN RUN MORE THAN 100 KILOMETRES (62 miles) PER HOUR!

All cats have NATURAL HUNTING instincts.

CATS HAVE PLAYED A PART IN THE

EXTINCTION

OF 33 DIFFERENT SPECIES OF ANIMAL.

Cats' claws all **POINT BACK** towards their limbs.

40

Because of the CURL in its claws, A CAT CAN'T CLIMB down a tree HEAD FIRST!

41

CATS can SURVIVE FALLS from HIGH UP.

Their bodies automatically TWIST AROUND to land on their FEET.

CATS CAN SQUEEZE INTO SMALL SPACES

BECAUSE THEY HAVE FREE-FLOATING CLAVICLES.

MOST CATS DON'T LIKE BEING IN WATER.

WET FUR can be HEAVY and COLD

Cats move their **RIGHT** feet first and then their **LEFT**.

46

GIRAFFES AND CAMELS ARE THE ONLY OTHER ANIMALS TO WALK THIS WAY.

A CAT CALLED JAKE HOLDS THE WORLD RECORD FOR THE MOST TOES.

HE HAS 28!

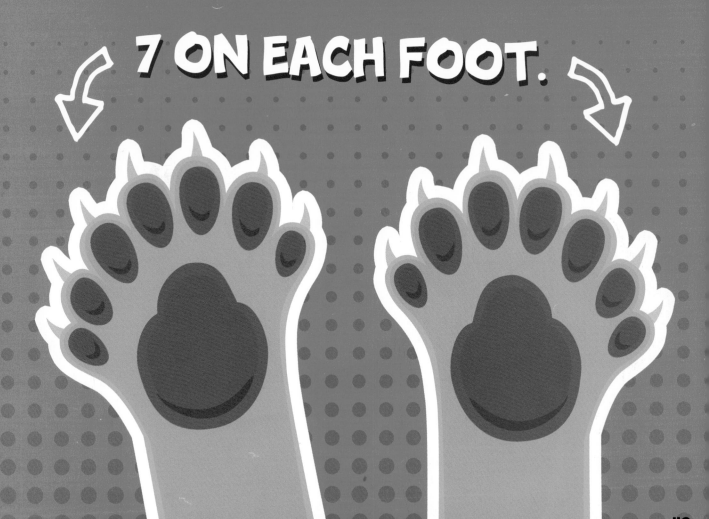

7 ON EACH FOOT.

THE FAMOUS AUTHOR ERNEST HEMINGWAY HAD A POLYDACTYL CAT.

That's a cat with EXTRA toes!

A GROWTH HORMONE IS RELEASED WHEN A KITTEN IS SLEEPING.

zzZZZZ

CATS SLEEP FOR ABOUT 70% OF THEIR LIVES.

That's 16 hours per day of beauty sleep!

UP TO
50%
OF A CAT'S
WAKING HOURS
ARE SPENT
CLEANING
ITSELF.

UNLIKE HUMANS, CATS CAN DRINK SOME SALT WATER.

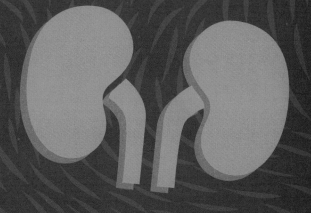

THEIR KIDNEYS FILTER OUT THE SALT.

YOU ACTUALLY SHOULDN'T GIVE YOUR CAT MILK!

MOST CATS ARE LACTOSE INTOLERANT!

CATS HAVE AN EXTRA ORGAN THAT LETS THEM 'TASTE' THE AIR.

It is called the Jacobson's organ.

CATS CANNOT TASTE SWEETS.

THE BUMPS

ON A CAT'S NOSE ARE

UNIQUE

TO EACH CAT.

They are like a
human's fingerprint.

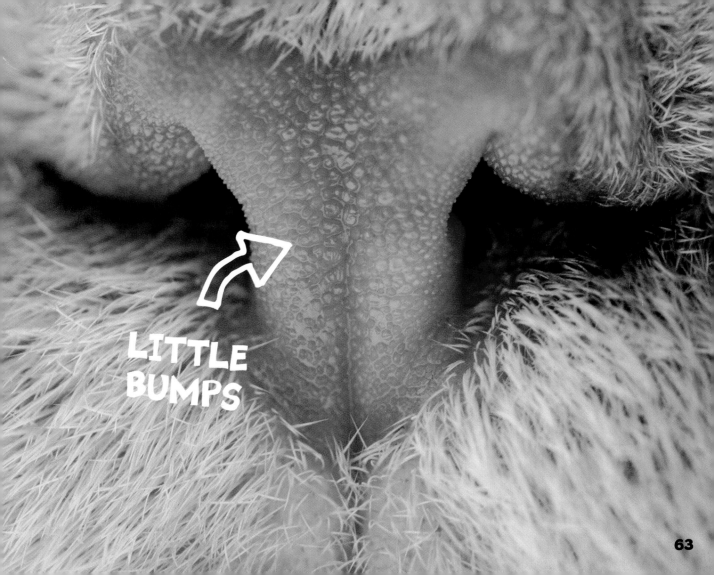

LITTLE
BUMPS

CATS CAN'T SEE DIRECTLY IN FRONT OF OR BELOW THEIR NOSES.

A CAT'S EYE HAS THREE EYELIDS.

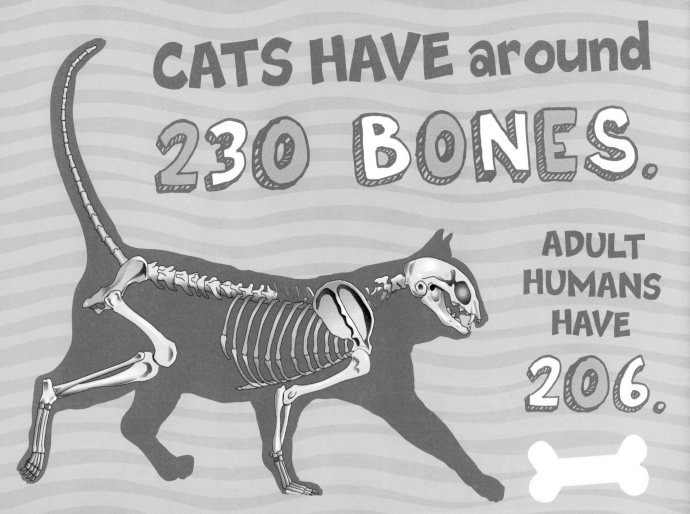

CATS HAVE around 230 BONES.

ADULT HUMANS HAVE 206.

ADULT CATS HAVE 30 TEETH.

WHISKERS help cats determine if they can FIT INTO A SPACE.

A CAT'S WHISKERS TYPICALLY GROW TO BE AS LONG AS THE CAT IS WIDE.

FAT CAT = LONG WHISKERS!

MOST CATS HAVE STRIPES, SPOTS OR ROSETTES.

ALBINO CATS are **RARE.** They are born without **PIGMENTATION (COLOUR).**

FEMALE feral cats often stay in small groups.

MALES are typically alone.

CATS HAVE SWEAT GLANDS IN THEIR PAWS.

These GLANDS also give off a

SCENT

that cats use to mark their TERRITORY.

MOST FEMALE CATS ARE RIGHT-PAWED.

MOST MALE CATS ARE LEFT-PAWED.

A FEMALE CAT is called a **QUEEN** or a **MOLLY.**

A MALE CAT is called a **TOM.**

'KITTY'

IS ONE OF THE TOP CAT NAMES.

KITTY

A LITTER is a group of kittens born at the same time.

LITTER is also what some pet cats **WEE** and **POO** in.

AN AILUROPHILE IS A CAT LOVER.

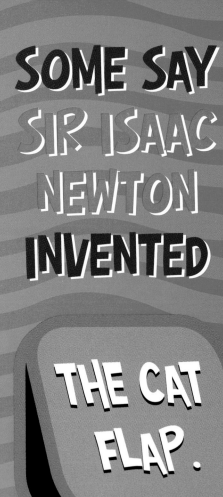

SOME SAY SIR ISAAC NEWTON INVENTED

THE CAT FLAP.

84

It is believed he may have cut a flap for a **MOTHER CAT** and, of course, a smaller flap for **HER KITTENS**.

US PRESIDENT LINCOLN WAS A CAT LOVER AND OFTEN BROUGHT HOME STRAYS.

TABBY and **DIXIE**, two of President Lincoln's cats, often ate **AT THE DINNER TABLE!**

Owning a CAT LOWERS a person's RISK of having a STROKE or HEART ATTACK.

SOME PEOPLE CONSIDER **BLACK CATS** TO BE **BAD LUCK.**

OTHERS THINK BLACK CATS BRING GOOD LUCK.

Disneyland has more than 200 CATS.

THE CATS
HUNT MICE
IN THE PARK
AT NIGHT.

CAT ISLAND

HUNDREDS OF CATS LIVE ON AN ISLAND IN JAPAN.

The human residents have created a cat shrine in the middle of the island.

CIVET CATS in Southeast Asia and Africa **EAT**

COFFEE BERRIES.

People use the undigested berry beans from the cats' poo to make

COFFEE.

STUBBS THE CAT

was **MAYOR** of Talkeetna, Alaska, USA, for **20 YEARS**.

His office was at Nagley's Store.

GRUMPY CAT

WENT VIRAL IN 2012.

HER FROWNY FACE
MADE HER
AN INTERNET HIT.

SHE HAS BEEN THE FEATURE OF MANY MEMES.

A CAT CALLED

SOPHIE SMITH

HAS THE

LONGEST FUR

OF ANY CAT.

Her fur is
25.68 CENTIMETRES
(10.11 INCHES)
LONG!

☆ LIL BUB ☆

IS A PERMA-KITTEN.

She will have **KITTEN FEATURES** for her **ENTIRE LIFE.** Her lower jaw is shorter than her top jaw, and she still has kitten teeth.

FELICETTE

ALSO KNOWN AS 'ASTROCAT'

WAS THE

FIRST CAT
IN OUTER
SPACE.

She was in space for **15 MINUTES** before returning to Earth.

I'm a **STAR!**

▶ MARU ◀

is a **SCOTTISH FOLD CAT**
that lives in **JAPAN**.
His **YOUTUBE** videos
have been viewed over

**325 MILLION
TIMES!**

GLOSSARY

clavicle bone between the shoulder and neck

communicate share information, thoughts or feelings

determine decide on something after giving it some thought

domesticate tame an animal so that it can live with or be used by humans

extinction process of a species dying out

lactose intolerant when the body cannot digest sugars that are mainly found in milk and dairy products

meme video, photo or piece of text that is shared on the internet

mourn be very sad and miss a loved one who has died

mummify preserve a body with special salts and cloth to make it last for a very long time

polydactyl having more than the normal amount of fingers or toes

resident person that lives in one particular place

rosette rose-like markings on the fur and skin of some animals

shrine holy building or structure

territory area of land that an animal claims as its own to live in

viral rapid spreading of information on the internet

BOOKS

Cat Speak: Revealing Answers to the Strangest Cat Behaviours (Cats Rule), Maureen Webster (Raintree, 2016)

Cheetahs (Living in the Wild: Big Cats), Charlotte Guillain (Raintree, 2015)

Cool Cat Projects (Pet Projects), Isabel Thomas (Raintree, 2016)

The Everything Book of Cats and Kittens, Andrea Mills (DK Children, 2018)

WEBSITES

Find out more about the cheetah.
www.dkfindout.com/uk/animals-and-nature/cats/cheetah

Read six facts about cats.
www.dkfindout.com/uk/explore/6-facts-about-cats

INDEX

Raintree is an imprint of Capstone Global Library Limited, a company incorporated in England and Wales having its registered office at 264 Banbury Road, Oxford, OX2 7DY – Registered company number: 6695582

www.raintree.co.uk
myorders@raintree.co.uk

Text © Capstone Global Library Limited 2019
The moral rights of the proprietor have been asserted.

Original illustrations © Capstone Global Library Ltd
Originated by Capstone Global Library Ltd
Printed and bound in India

ISBN 978 1 4747 6564 0
22 21 20 19 18
10 9 8 7 6 5 4 3 2 1

British Library Cataloguing in Publication Data
A full catalogue record for this book is available from the British Library.

Acknowledgements
We would like to thank the following for permission to reproduce photographs:
Shutterstock: Tuzemka, cover (top left), Ermolaev Alexander, cover (top right), Eric Isselee, cover (bottom left), Ronnachai Palas, cover (bottom right) Ronaldino, 2, Susan Schmitz, 3, Eric Isselee, 5 (lion), Nikolai Tsvetkov, 6 (cat statue), WitR, 6 (pyramids), MasaMima, 7, Jason Stitt, 9, Vivienstock, 10, Martin Mecnarowski, 12, Jiri Vaclavek, 13), Callahan, 14 (maine Greeting), DragoNika, 14 (maine cat), Eric Isselee, 15 (maine cat), sagir, 15 (chair), beachbassman, 16, Linn Currie, 17, Eric Isselee, 18, Sari ONeal, 20, Petr Toman, 21, Laborant, 22, Siwaporn Yaweerah, 23, kvsan, 24 (money), MirasWonderland, 24 (black cat), Ermolaev Alexander, 26 (cat), hidesy, 26 (crown), Vadarshop, 26 (cushion), Ermolaev Alexander, 28, Margaret Jone Wollman, 29, 5 second Studio, 30, Tony Campbell, 31, Eric Isselee, 32, Valentina Razumova, 33, Ermolaev Alexander, 34, Srijaroen, 35, donikz, 36, Marcel Brekelmans, 37, Budimir Jevtic, 38, Lubava, 40, Ares Jonekson, 41, GraphiTect, 42 (sky), fantom_rd, 42 (flying kitten), Lario, 43, White bear studio, 44, Ukki Studio, 45, Eric Isselee, 46, Patryk Kosmider, 47 (camel), Eric Isselee, 47 (giraffe), Fotoluminate LLC, 50 (hemingway); Eric Isselee, 51, choikh, 52, Ermolaev Alexander, 53, Natthawut Chongvilaiwan, 54 (sleeping cat), kuban_girl, 54 (cat dressed up), Axel Bueckert, 55, MUANGPAI PHOTOGRAPHY, 56, Winston Link, 58, Dmitri Ma, 59, Ekaterina Kolomeets, 60 Kateryna Yakovlieva, 63, Lapina, 64, vladimir salman, 65, lexonline, 66, jorge pereira, 67, fantom_rd, 68, Utekhina Anna, 70, Eric Isselee, 72, Gelpi, 73, catinsyrup, 74, Seregraff, 77, DR-images, 78 (crown), Scorpp, 78 (cat girl), Kasefoto, 78 (cat boy), Africa Studio, 79, absolutimages, 80, Dmitrij Skorobogatov, 81, hawaya, 82, MatiasDelCarmine, 84, happymay, 85, Everett Historical, 86 (President Lincoln), Suzanne Tucker, 86 (cat 1), MirasWonderland, 86 (cat 2), Susan Schmitz, 86 (cat 3), mik ulyannikov, 87, 5 second Studio, 88, chrisbrignell, 89, MaraZe, 90, Kachalkina Veronika, 92 (wizard cat), Hedzun Vasyl, 92 (ribbon cat), sido kagawa, 94, LoulouVonGlup, 95, reptiles4all, 96 (coffee cat), NIPAPORN PANYACHAROEN, 96 (coffee berries), Kaiskynet Studio, 97 (coffee pooh), S.Bachstroem, 97 (coffee cup), TeddyandMia, 98 (mountains), shtiel, 98 (cat), LiveStock, 98 (banners/rosette), Jaguar PS, 101, Massimo Cattaneo, 102, Featureflash Photo Agency, 104, nienora, 107 (space), Olena Yakobchuk, 107 (astronaut), Erik Lam, 107 (cat), mdmmikle, 108; Getty/Getty/DigitalVision Vectors: THEPALMER, 4 (Noahs Arc); iStock/Getty Images Plus: c-foto, 4 (flying cats), Preto_perola, 4 (picture frame), Preto_perola, 50 (picture frame), Preto_perola, 86 (picture frame); Getty/E+: jkitan, 76 (cat paw);

Design Elements by Shutterstock, Getty Images and DynamoLimited

Every effort has been made to contact copyright holders of material reproduced in this book. Any omissions will be rectified in subsequent printings if notice is given to the publisher.

All the internet addresses (URLs) given in this book were valid at the time of going to press. However, due to the dynamic nature of the internet, some addresses may have changed, or sites may have changed or ceased to exist since publication.While the author and publisher regret any inconvenience this may cause readers, no responsibility for any such changes can be accepted by either the author or the publisher.